BUSINESS AND ENTREPRENEURSHIP

Introduction:

Are you interested in starting your own business or taking your existing business to the next level? Do you want to learn more about the key principles of entrepreneurship and how to apply them to your own situation? If so, then this book is for you.

In this book, we'll cover a range of topics related to business and entrepreneurship, from starting a business and marketing to sales and leadership. We'll provide practical tips and advice to help you succeed in your career or take your business to the next level.

As an entrepreneur myself, I understand the challenges and opportunities that come with starting and growing a business. Over the years, I've learned what works and what doesn't, and I'm excited to share that knowledge with you.

Whether you're just starting out or looking for ways to improve your existing business, this book will provide you with the guidance and inspiration you need to succeed. So, let's dive in and explore the exciting world of business and entrepreneurship together.

CHAPTER 1: STARTING A BUSINESS

- Importance of having a clear vision and mission for your business
- Steps involved in creating a business plan
- Practical tips for identifying your target market and assessing the competition
- Different business structures and the pros and cons of each
- Funding options for startups

CHAPTER 2: MARKETING

- Importance of marketing in attracting and retaining customers
- Different marketing strategies, including social media, email marketing, and content marketing
- Practical tips for creating a strong brand identity and messaging
- Role of market research in developing effective marketing campaigns

CHAPTER 3: SALES

- Basics of sales, including prospecting, qualifying leads, and closing deals
- Practical tips for building rapport with customers and overcoming objections
- Importance of customer relationship management and how to do it effectively
- Role of data analysis in optimizing sales performance

CHAPTER 4: LEADERSHIP

- Importance of strong leadership in business success
- Traits and skills of effective leaders
- Practical tips for developing leadership skills, including communication, delegation, and decision-making
- Role of emotional intelligence in effective leadership

CHAPTER 5: OPERATIONS AND MANAGEMENT

- Importance of effective operations and management in business success
- Practical tips for managing finances, inventory, and other resources
- Importance of continuous improvement and how to implement it in your business
- Role of technology in streamlining operations and improving efficiency

CHAPTER 1: STARTING A BUSINESS

Importance of having a clear vision and mission for your business

Having a clear vision and mission is critical for any business, as it provides direction and purpose for all stakeholders involved, including employees, customers, investors, and partners. Here are some key reasons why having a clear vision and mission is essential for business success:

Provides direction: A clear vision and mission statement outline the long-term goals and purpose of the business. This helps to provide direction to employees, who can align their work towards achieving the company's goals. It also helps to guide decision-making, as all choices can be evaluated in the context of the company's vision and mission.

Builds culture and values: A vision and mission statement can also help to build a strong culture and values within the organization. When employees are clear about the company's values and purpose, they are more likely to feel a sense of belonging and commitment to the company's success.

Attracts customers: A clear and compelling vision and mission can also help to attract customers who share the same values and beliefs. Customers want to do business with companies that align with their own values and beliefs, and a clear vision and mission statement can communicate this effectively.

Differentiates the business: In a crowded marketplace, having a clear vision and mission statement can help to differentiate the business from competitors. When customers and investors can clearly understand the company's purpose and values, they are more likely to choose that business over others.

In summary, having a clear vision and mission statement is essential for business success. It provides direction, builds culture and values, attracts customers, and differentiates the business. As an entrepreneur, it's important to take the time to create a compelling vision and mission statement that reflects the purpose and values of your business.

Steps involved in creating a business plan

Here's an outline of the steps involved in creating a business plan:

Executive Summary: This is a brief overview of your business, including the company's mission statement, the products or services you offer, the market you serve, and your financial projections.

Company Description: This section provides a more detailed description of your business, including your business structure, legal entity, ownership, location, and history.

Market Analysis: This section outlines the market and industry you're operating in, including market size, trends, and competition.

Products and Services: This section details the products and services you offer, their unique features, and the benefits they provide to customers.

Marketing and Sales: This section describes how you plan to market and sell your products and services, including your target audience, pricing strategy, distribution channels, and promotional tactics.

Operations: This section details the day-to-day operations of your business, including production, logistics, inventory management, and quality control.

Management and Organization: This section outlines the organizational structure of your business, including the management team, key personnel, and their roles and responsibilities.

Financials: This section includes financial projections, including income statements, balance sheets, cash flow statements, and break-even analysis. It also includes a discussion of your funding needs, how you plan to use the funds, and your expected return on investment.

Appendix: This section includes any supporting documents, such as resumes of key personnel, market research data, and legal documents.

Creating a business plan can be a time-consuming process, but it's an essential step for any entrepreneur who wants to start or grow a successful business. By following these steps and providing a clear, concise, and compelling business plan, you can increase your chances of securing funding, attracting customers, and achieving your business goals.

Practical tips for identifying your target market and assessing the competition

Here are some practical tips for identifying your target market and assessing the competition:

Identifying Your Target Market:

Conduct Market Research: Use online tools, surveys, focus groups, and other research methods to gather information about your potential customers. This will help you to understand their needs, preferences, and behavior.

Analyze Demographics: Look at the age, gender, income,

education, and other characteristics of your potential customers. This will help you to segment your market and identify specific groups of people who are most likely to be interested in your product or service.

Consider Psychographics: In addition to demographics, look at the values, attitudes, and lifestyles of your potential customers. This will help you to understand their motivations and preferences, and tailor your marketing message accordingly.

Identify Pain Points: Determine the problems or challenges your potential customers are facing, and how your product or service can solve these problems. This will help you to create a targeted marketing message that resonates with your audience.

Assessing the Competition:

Identify Competitors: Research your competitors to understand their strengths, weaknesses, and marketing strategies. Look at their products or services, pricing, distribution channels, and marketing messages.

Conduct SWOT Analysis: Analyze your own business and your competitors using a SWOT (strengths, weaknesses, opportunities, and threats) analysis. This will help you to identify your own strengths and weaknesses, as well as potential opportunities and threats in the market.

Determine Unique Selling Proposition (USP): Identify what sets your product or service apart from your competitors. This could be features, benefits, pricing, or other factors that differentiate your product from the competition.

Monitor and Adjust: Keep an eye on your competitors and adjust your marketing strategies as needed. This could include changing your pricing, improving your product or service, or finding new marketing channels to reach your target audience.

By identifying your target market and assessing the competition, you can develop a marketing strategy that resonates with your audience and sets your business apart from the competition.

Different business structures and the pros and cons of each

Sure, here are some of the different business structures and their pros and cons:

Sole Proprietorship: A sole proprietorship is a business owned and operated by a single individual. It is the simplest and least expensive form of business structure.

Pros:

Easy and inexpensive to set up and operate

Full control over the business

Personal tax rates apply, which can be lower than corporate tax rates

Cons:

Unlimited personal liability for business debts and legal issues

Limited ability to raise capital

Limited lifespan and difficult to transfer ownership

Partnership: A partnership is a business structure in which two or more people share ownership and management of the business.

Pros:

Shared responsibility, workload, and risk

Easy and inexpensive to set up and operate

Personal tax rates apply, which can be lower than corporate tax rates

Cons:

Unlimited personal liability for business debts and legal issues

Limited ability to raise capital

Limited lifespan and difficult to transfer ownership

Limited Liability Company (LLC): A limited liability company (LLC) is a hybrid business structure that provides the flexibility of a partnership with the liability protection of a corporation.

Pros:

Limited liability for business debts and legal issues

Flexible management structure

Pass-through taxation (profits are taxed at personal tax rates)

Cons:

More expensive to set up and operate than a sole proprietorship or partnership

Complexity of operation and regulation

Limited lifespan and difficult to transfer ownership

Corporation: A corporation is a separate legal entity that is owned by shareholders and managed by a board of directors.

Pros:

Limited liability for shareholders

Ability to raise capital through sale of stocks and bonds

Perpetual lifespan and ease of ownership transfer

Cons:

More expensive and complex to set up and operate

Double taxation (profits are taxed at the corporate and personal levels)

Increased regulation and reporting requirements

Choosing the right business structure is an important decision that will have long-term implications for your business. Careful consideration of the pros and cons of each structure can help you to make an informed decision that best meets the needs of your business.

Funding options for startups

Here are some funding options for startups:

Bootstrapping: Bootstrapping is a method of funding your startup by using your own personal savings, credit cards, or other resources to get the business off the ground.

Pros:

No debt or outside equity

Retain full control over the business

Lower risk of dilution of ownership

Cons:

Limited resources may hinder growth and expansion

High personal financial risk

Difficulty in attracting outside investors in the future

Friends and Family: Friends and family can be a potential source of funding for your startup. This could include loans or investments from family members, close friends, or acquaintances.

Pros:

Easy access to capital

Lower cost of capital

Support from people who know and believe in you

Cons:

Personal relationships can be strained if the business fails

Limited resources may hinder growth and expansion

Lack of professional guidance and oversight

Crowdfunding: Crowdfunding is a method of raising funds from a large number of people, typically through an online platform.

Pros:

Access to a large pool of potential investors

Opportunity for marketing and promotion of the business

Limited financial risk for the entrepreneur

Cons:

Competition with other crowdfunding campaigns

Time-consuming and requires marketing efforts

Limited amount of funding

Angel Investors: Angel investors are high-net-worth individuals who invest in early-stage startups in exchange for equity.

Pros:

Access to larger amounts of capital

Professional guidance and expertise from investors

Potential for networking and business opportunities

Cons:

Dilution of ownership and control

High expectations for return on investment

Limited availability of investors in some geographic areas

Venture Capital: Venture capital is a form of private equity financing that provides funding to high-growth startups in exchange for equity.

Pros:

Access to large amounts of capital

Professional guidance and expertise from investors

Potential for networking and business opportunities

Cons:

Dilution of ownership and control

High expectations for return on investment

Limited availability of investors for early-stage startups

Choosing the right funding option for your startup depends on a variety of factors, including the stage of your business, the amount of funding required, and your long-term goals. Careful consideration of the pros and cons of each option can help you to make an informed decision that best meets the needs of your business.

CHAPTER 2: MARKETING

Importance of marketing in attracting and retaining customers

Marketing is critical for attracting and retaining customers because it helps businesses to communicate their brand, products or services, and value proposition to potential customers. Here are some specific reasons why marketing is important for businesses:

Building brand awareness: Marketing helps to create brand awareness and make customers aware of your business, products or services. This is particularly important for startups and small businesses that are new to the market and need to establish a presence.

Attracting new customers: Marketing is essential for attracting new customers to your business. By identifying your target market and developing effective marketing strategies, you can reach out to potential customers and encourage them to try your products or services.

Increasing customer loyalty: Effective marketing can help to build customer loyalty by creating a positive impression of your business and products or services. By engaging with customers through marketing campaigns, you can build strong relationships that encourage repeat business and referrals.

Staying ahead of the competition: Marketing helps businesses to stay ahead of the competition by identifying and leveraging unique selling propositions, or USPs, that differentiate their products or services from those of their competitors. By developing effective marketing strategies that highlight these USPs, businesses can attract and retain customers more effectively.

Generating revenue: Ultimately, the purpose of marketing is to generate revenue for the business. By attracting and retaining customers through effective marketing campaigns, businesses can increase sales and grow their revenue over time.

In summary, marketing plays a critical role in attracting and retaining customers by building brand awareness, attracting new customers, increasing customer loyalty, staying ahead of the competition, and generating revenue for the business. By investing in marketing efforts that are tailored to the needs of your business and target market, you can establish a strong presence in the market and achieve long-term success.

Different marketing strategies, including social media, email marketing, and content marketing

There are many marketing strategies that businesses can use to reach their target audience and build their brand. Here are some of the most popular and effective marketing strategies, including social media marketing, email marketing, and content marketing:

Social Media Marketing: Social media marketing involves using social media platforms like Facebook, Instagram, Twitter, and LinkedIn to promote a business and its products or services. This strategy involves creating engaging content that resonates with the target audience, building a community of followers, and using paid advertising to reach a wider audience.

Pros:

Wide reach to a large audience

Cost-effective compared to other forms of advertising

Ability to engage directly with customers and build relationships

Cons:

High competition for attention on social media

Requires ongoing effort to maintain engagement

Risk of negative feedback or backlash

Email Marketing: Email marketing involves using email to communicate with customers and promote a business and its products or services. This strategy involves building an email list of subscribers, creating engaging content that resonates with the target audience, and using automation to send targeted messages at the right time.

Pros:

Highly targeted and personalized messaging

Cost-effective compared to other forms of advertising

Ability to measure and analyze results

Cons:

Risk of emails being marked as spam

Requires a consistent schedule to maintain engagement

Risk of unsubscribes or low open rates

Content Marketing: Content marketing involves creating valuable and informative content that resonates with the target audience and helps to position the business as an authority in its industry. This strategy involves creating blog posts, videos, infographics, and other forms of content that educate and inform the target audience.

Pros:

Builds trust and credibility with the target audience

Helps to position the business as an authority in its industry

Provides value to the target audience even before they become customers

Cons:

Requires a significant investment of time and resources

Results may take time to materialize

Risk of creating content that does not resonate with the target audience

These are just a few examples of marketing strategies that businesses can use to reach their target audience and build their brand. It's important to choose the strategies that are most effective for your business and target audience, and to continually test and refine your marketing efforts over time to achieve the best results.

Practical tips for creating a strong brand identity and messaging

A strong brand identity and messaging are critical for businesses to stand out in a crowded market and connect with their target audience. Here are some practical tips for creating a strong brand identity and messaging:

Define your brand values and personality: Before you can create a strong brand identity and messaging, it's important to define your brand values and personality. This involves identifying the unique characteristics that set your brand apart from the competition, and the values that you want to communicate to your target audience.

Develop a consistent visual identity: Consistency is key when it comes to branding, and this applies to your visual identity as well. Develop a visual identity that reflects your brand values and personality, including colors, fonts, and other design elements.

Create a strong brand voice: Your brand voice is the tone and style of your messaging, and it should reflect your brand values and personality. Consider the language and tone that will resonate with your target audience, and develop messaging that is consistent across all channels.

Use storytelling to connect with your audience: Storytelling is a powerful tool for creating a strong brand identity and messaging. Use storytelling to communicate your brand values and personality, and to connect with your target audience on an emotional level.

Consistently reinforce your brand messaging: Consistency is key when it comes to branding, so it's important to reinforce your brand messaging across all channels. This includes your website, social media, advertising, and other marketing efforts.

Test and refine your messaging: Finally, it's important to continually test and refine your brand messaging to ensure that it resonates with your target audience. Use data and feedback to refine your messaging over time, and adjust your strategy as needed to achieve the best results.

By following these practical tips, businesses can create a strong brand identity and messaging that resonates with their target audience and sets them apart from the competition.

Role of market research in developing effective marketing campaigns

Market research plays a critical role in developing effective marketing campaigns by providing businesses with insights into their target audience, their needs and preferences, and the competitive landscape. Here are some ways market research can inform marketing campaigns:

Identify target audience: Market research helps businesses to identify their target audience by gathering information about their demographics, psychographics, behaviors, and preferences. This information helps businesses to tailor their marketing messages and strategies to the specific needs and interests of their target audience.

Understand customer needs and preferences: Market research can also provide businesses with insights into their customers' needs and preferences. This helps businesses to develop products and services that meet the needs of their target audience, and to create marketing messages that resonate with them.

Evaluate the competitive landscape: Market research can also help businesses to understand the competitive landscape and identify opportunities for differentiation. By understanding their competitors' strengths and weaknesses, businesses can position themselves in a way that sets them apart from the competition.

Measure the effectiveness of marketing campaigns: Market research can also be used to measure the effectiveness of marketing campaigns. By gathering feedback from customers and monitoring key metrics such as engagement, conversions, and sales, businesses can evaluate the success of their marketing campaigns and make adjustments as needed.

In summary, market research provides businesses with valuable insights into their target audience, their needs and preferences, and the competitive landscape. This information can be used to develop effective marketing campaigns that resonate with customers and set businesses apart from the competition.

CHAPTER 3: SALES

Basics of sales, including prospecting, qualifying leads, and closing deals

Sales is the process of identifying, contacting, and converting potential customers into paying customers. It involves several stages, including prospecting, qualifying leads, and closing deals. Here are some basics of each stage:

Prospecting: Prospecting involves identifying potential customers who may be interested in your products or services. This can be done through various methods, such as cold calling, email marketing, social media outreach, and networking. The goal of prospecting is to generate a list of potential customers who can be further qualified.

Qualifying leads: Once you have a list of potential customers, the next step is to qualify them. This involves gathering more information about their needs, budget, decision-making process, and timeline. The goal of qualifying leads is to determine whether they are a good fit for your products or services, and whether they are ready to make a purchase.

Closing deals: Closing deals is the final stage of the sales process, and involves converting qualified leads into paying customers. This can be done through various methods, such as presenting a proposal, negotiating terms, and addressing any objections or concerns. The goal of closing deals is to reach an agreement that is mutually beneficial for both parties.

Tips for each stage of the sales process:

Prospecting:

Focus on quality over quantity when identifying potential customers.

Tailor your messaging and approach to the specific needs and interests of your target audience.

Use a mix of outreach methods to maximize your reach and engagement.

Qualifying leads:

Ask open-ended questions to gather more information about your prospects.

Listen actively to understand their needs and concerns.

Determine whether they have the budget, authority, need, and timeline to make a purchase.

Closing deals:

Build rapport and trust with your prospects throughout the sales process.

Address any objections or concerns that may arise.

Present your proposal in a clear and compelling way, emphasizing the value and benefits of your products or services.

In summary, sales is a critical function for businesses, and involves several stages, including prospecting, qualifying leads, and closing deals. By mastering these basics and following best practices, businesses can increase their sales and grow their customer base.

Practical tips for building rapport with customers and overcoming objections

Building rapport with customers and overcoming objections are two key skills that salespeople need to master in order to be successful. Here are some practical tips for each:

Building rapport with customers:

Listen actively: Show your customers that you care about their needs and concerns by actively listening to what they have to say.

Ask open-ended questions: Encourage your customers to share more about their needs and interests by asking open-ended questions that require more than a yes or no answer.

Use positive body language: Smile, maintain eye contact, and use open gestures to convey warmth and openness.

Find common ground: Look for shared interests or experiences that you can use to build a connection with your customers.

Follow up: Show your customers that you value their business by following up with them after a sale or meeting.

Overcoming objections:

Anticipate objections: Before a sales call or meeting, try to anticipate any objections that a customer may have and prepare responses in advance.

Address objections head-on: When a customer raises an objection, address it directly and provide a clear and concise response.

Focus on benefits: Emphasize the benefits of your products or services and how they can address the customer's needs and concerns.

Use social proof: Share case studies or testimonials from satisfied customers to demonstrate the value and effectiveness of your products or services.

Show empathy: Acknowledge the customer's concerns and show empathy for their situation.

In summary, building rapport with customers and overcoming objections are critical skills for salespeople. By listening actively, asking open-ended questions, using positive body language, anticipating objections, and focusing on benefits, salespeople can build trust and credibility with their customers and increase their chances of closing a deal.

Importance of customer relationship management and on how to do it effectively

Customer relationship management (CRM) is a vital aspect of any business that seeks to build long-term, profitable relationships with its customers. Effective CRM helps businesses to understand and anticipate their customers' needs, and to provide them with personalized experiences that enhance their loyalty and satisfaction. Here are some tips for effective CRM:

Collect and analyze customer data: Collect as much data as possible about your customers, including their contact information, purchase history, and feedback. Analyze this data to identify trends and patterns that can help you to better understand their needs and preferences.

Segment your customer base: Divide your customers into different segments based on factors such as demographics, buying behavior, and interests. This will allow you to tailor your marketing and customer service efforts to each group.

Provide excellent customer service: Respond promptly to customer inquiries, complaints, and feedback, and go above and beyond to meet their needs and expectations. This will help to build trust and loyalty.

Offer personalized experiences: Use customer data to provide personalized recommendations and experiences that meet each customer's unique needs and preferences.

Use automation tools: Use CRM software and automation tools to streamline your customer service and marketing efforts, and to track interactions with each customer.

Continuously improve: Regularly solicit feedback from customers and use this feedback to improve your products, services, and customer experiences.

In summary, effective CRM requires businesses to collect and analyze customer data, segment their customer base, provide excellent customer service, offer personalized experiences, use automation tools, and continuously improve. By following these tips, businesses can build strong, long-term relationships with their customers and increase their chances of success.

Role of data analysis in optimizing sales performance

Data analysis plays a critical role in optimizing sales performance by helping businesses to understand their customers' needs and preferences, identify trends and patterns in sales data, and measure the effectiveness of sales strategies and tactics. Here are some ways that data analysis can help businesses to optimize their sales performance:

Customer segmentation: By analyzing customer data, businesses can identify different segments of customers based on factors such as demographics, buying behavior, and interests. This allows them to tailor their sales strategies and tactics to each group, improving the effectiveness of their sales efforts.

Sales forecasting: Data analysis can help businesses to forecast sales volumes and revenue based on historical data and current market trends. This enables businesses to plan and allocate resources more effectively and make informed decisions about future sales strategies and investments.

Sales performance measurement: By analyzing sales data, businesses can measure the performance of their sales teams and individual sales reps, identifying areas of strength and weakness. This allows them to provide targeted training and support to improve sales performance and achieve better results.

Sales funnel analysis: By analyzing sales funnel data, businesses can identify bottlenecks and areas of inefficiency in their sales process, and make data-driven improvements to optimize the process and improve sales conversion rates.

Marketing campaign analysis: By analyzing data from marketing campaigns, businesses can measure the effectiveness of different marketing strategies and tactics, and optimize campaigns to maximize ROI.

In summary, data analysis plays a crucial role in optimizing sales performance by helping businesses to identify customer segments, forecast sales volumes, measure sales performance, analyze the sales funnel, and optimize marketing campaigns. By leveraging data to inform sales strategies and tactics, businesses can improve their sales performance and achieve better results.

CHAPTER 4: LEADERSHIP

Importance of strong leadership in business success

Strong leadership is a critical factor in the success of any business, as it sets the tone for the organization and shapes its culture, values, and priorities. Effective leaders inspire their teams, set clear goals and expectations, make tough decisions, and drive innovation and growth. Here are some key reasons why strong leadership is important for business success:

Sets a clear direction: Strong leaders have a clear vision for the business and can communicate this vision effectively to their teams. This helps to align everyone in the organization around common goals and priorities, and ensures that everyone is working towards the same objectives.

Builds a strong culture: Leaders shape the culture of the organization by modeling desired behaviors and values, setting expectations for performance and accountability, and fostering a positive and inclusive work environment. This can help to attract and retain top talent and create a high-performing team.

Drives innovation and growth: Effective leaders encourage innovation and creativity by empowering their teams to take risks and try new things. They also foster a culture of continuous improvement and learning, which can lead to new ideas, products, and services that drive growth and success.

Builds trust and credibility: Strong leaders build trust and credibility with their teams and stakeholders by being transparent, honest, and accountable. They communicate clearly and authentically, and follow through on their commitments, which helps to establish a culture of trust and respect.

Manages change and uncertainty: Leaders are often called upon to manage change and uncertainty, such as during times of economic upheaval, technological disruption, or organizational restructuring. Strong leaders are able to adapt to changing circumstances, make tough decisions, and communicate clearly and effectively with their teams to help them navigate these challenges.

In summary, strong leadership is critical to the success of any business, as it sets the direction, builds a strong culture, drives innovation and growth, builds trust and credibility, and manages change and uncertainty. By cultivating strong leadership skills and building a culture of excellence, businesses can increase their chances of success and thrive in today's competitive marketplace.

Traits and skills of effective leaders

Effective leaders possess a wide range of traits and skills that enable them to inspire and guide their teams towards success. Here are some key traits and skills that are commonly associated with effective leaders:

Vision: Effective leaders have a clear vision for the future of their organization and are able to communicate this vision to their teams in a way that inspires and motivates them.

Communication: Effective leaders are skilled communicators who are able to articulate their vision, expectations, and feedback clearly and respectfully.

Empathy: Effective leaders are empathetic and able to understand the perspectives and needs of their team members. They are able to listen actively and respond with compassion and understanding.

Decisiveness: Effective leaders are able to make tough decisions quickly and confidently, while also weighing risks and considering multiple options.

Adaptability: Effective leaders are adaptable and able to respond to changing circumstances and challenges. They are able to pivot quickly and adjust their strategies and plans as needed.

Accountability: Effective leaders hold themselves and their team members accountable for their actions and outcomes. They are willing to take responsibility for mistakes and work with their teams to learn from them.

Integrity: Effective leaders act with integrity, honesty, and ethics. They model positive behavior and hold themselves to high standards of conduct.

Strategic thinking: Effective leaders are strategic thinkers who are able to see the big picture and think critically about how to achieve their goals. They are able to anticipate challenges and opportunities and plan accordingly.

Empowerment: Effective leaders empower their team members to take ownership of their work and contribute to the success of the organization. They provide opportunities for growth and development and encourage creativity and innovation.

In summary, effective leaders possess a wide range of traits and skills, including vision, communication, empathy, decisiveness, adaptability, accountability, integrity, strategic thinking, and empowerment. By cultivating these skills and traits, leaders can inspire and guide their teams towards success and create a culture of excellence within their organization.

Practical tips for developing leadership skills, including communication, delegation, and decision-making

Developing leadership skills is an ongoing process that requires practice, self-reflection, and a willingness to learn and grow. Here are some practical tips for developing key leadership skills:

Communication: To improve your communication skills, practice active listening, ask open-ended questions, and be mindful of your tone and body language. When giving feedback, use specific examples and be clear and concise.

Delegation: Delegation is a key skill for effective leadership. To improve your delegation skills, assess the strengths and weaknesses of your team members, communicate your expectations clearly, and provide the necessary resources and support.

Decision-making: To improve your decision-making skills, gather as much information as possible, consider multiple options, and weigh the risks and benefits of each. Trust your intuition, but also seek input from others and be open to feedback.

Emotional intelligence: Emotional intelligence is the ability to understand and manage your own emotions, as well as the emotions of others. To improve your emotional intelligence, practice mindfulness, empathy, and self-reflection.

Time management: Effective leaders are able to manage their time effectively to maximize their productivity and achieve their goals. To improve your time management skills, prioritize your tasks, set clear deadlines, and use tools like calendars and to-do lists to stay organized.

Conflict resolution: Conflict is inevitable in any workplace, but effective leaders are able to resolve conflicts in a way that is fair, respectful, and constructive. To improve your conflict resolution skills, listen to both sides of the story, identify the underlying issues, and work with both parties to find a solution.

Continuous learning: Effective leaders are committed to continuous learning and personal growth. To improve your leadership skills, seek feedback from others, attend workshops and training sessions, and read books and articles on leadership and management.

In summary, developing leadership skills requires a combination of practice, self-reflection, and a willingness to learn and grow. By focusing on communication, delegation, decision-making, emotional intelligence, time management, conflict resolution, and continuous learning, you can become a more effective and successful leader.

Role of emotional intelligence in effective leadership

Emotional intelligence is a critical component of effective leadership. It refers to the ability to understand and manage one's own emotions, as well as the emotions of others. Leaders with high emotional intelligence are able to build strong relationships, inspire and motivate their team, and navigate complex interpersonal dynamics.

Here are some specific ways that emotional intelligence can enhance leadership:

Building relationships: Leaders with high emotional intelligence are able to build strong relationships with their team members, customers, and other stakeholders. They are able to connect with people on an emotional level, which builds trust and fosters collaboration.

Empathy: Effective leaders are able to put themselves in others' shoes and understand their perspectives and feelings. This allows them to be more responsive to their team members' needs and concerns.

Conflict resolution: Leaders with high emotional intelligence are able to resolve conflicts in a way that is fair, respectful, and constructive. They are able to listen to both sides of the story and find solutions that satisfy everyone's needs.

Motivation: Emotional intelligence can help leaders motivate their team members by understanding what drives and inspires them. By tailoring their leadership style to each individual, leaders can create a more engaged and motivated team.

Communication: Leaders with high emotional intelligence are able to communicate effectively, using language that resonates with their team members and customers. They are able to read the emotional tone of a conversation and adjust their communication style accordingly.

In summary, emotional intelligence plays a critical role in effective leadership. By building relationships, showing empathy, resolving conflicts, motivating their team, and communicating effectively, leaders with high emotional intelligence can create a more positive and productive work environment.

CHAPTER 5: OPERATIONS AND MANAGEMENT

Importance of effective operations and management in business success

Effective operations and management are essential to business success for several reasons:

Efficient resource allocation: Effective operations and management ensure that resources are allocated efficiently, minimizing waste and maximizing productivity. This allows the business to operate more profitably, which is essential for long-term success.

Customer satisfaction: Operations and management play a key role in ensuring that customers receive products and services that meet their needs and expectations. A well-managed business will have effective processes in place to ensure consistent quality and timely delivery of products and services.

Employee engagement: Effective operations and management can help to engage employees by providing them with clear expectations and goals, as well as the tools and resources they need to succeed. This can lead to higher job satisfaction, productivity, and retention.

Adaptability: In today's fast-paced business environment, it is essential for businesses to be able to adapt quickly to changing circumstances. Effective operations and management can help to create a culture of agility and innovation, which allows businesses to respond quickly to changing market conditions.

Cost management: Effective operations and management are also critical for managing costs. By optimizing processes and minimizing waste, businesses can reduce their expenses and improve their bottom line.

In summary, effective operations and management are essential to business success. They ensure efficient resource allocation, customer satisfaction, employee engagement, adaptability, and cost management. By prioritizing operations and management, businesses can position themselves for long-term success in today's competitive marketplace.

Practical tips for managing finances, inventory, and other resources

Here are some practical tips for managing finances, inventory, and other resources in a business:

Develop a budget: Creating a budget is essential for managing finances effectively. A budget helps to identify revenue and expenses, and provides a framework for making decisions about how to allocate resources.

Monitor cash flow: Cash flow is the lifeblood of any business. To manage cash flow effectively, it is important to regularly monitor and analyze incoming and outgoing cash.

Control inventory: Effective inventory management involves finding the right balance between having enough inventory to meet demand, but not so much that it becomes a financial burden. To control inventory effectively, businesses should track inventory levels, set reorder points, and establish inventory turnover goals.

Negotiate payment terms: Negotiating payment terms with vendors and suppliers can help to improve cash flow and reduce the need for borrowing. For example, negotiating longer payment terms can provide additional time to pay invoices, while negotiating discounts for early payment can reduce the overall cost of goods.

Use technology: Technology can be a valuable tool for managing finances, inventory, and other resources. For example, accounting software can help to track expenses and revenue, while inventory management software can provide real-time data on inventory levels and demand.

Regularly review financial statements: Regularly reviewing financial statements is essential for understanding the financial health of a business. Financial statements provide insights into revenue, expenses, cash flow, and profitability, and can help to identify areas where improvements can be made.

By implementing these practical tips for managing finances, inventory, and other resources, businesses can position themselves for long-term success and growth.

Importance of continuous improvement and how to implement it in your business

Continuous improvement is the process of identifying areas where a business can improve and implementing changes to drive growth and success. It is important because it helps businesses stay competitive, adapt to changing market conditions, and meet the evolving needs of customers. Here are some tips on how to implement continuous improvement in your business:

Establish a culture of continuous improvement: Encourage employees to contribute ideas and suggestions for improvement, and make continuous improvement a part of the company culture.

Set goals and measure progress: Set measurable goals for improvement, and regularly measure progress to ensure that goals are being met.

Conduct regular evaluations: Conduct regular evaluations of business processes and systems to identify areas for improvement.

Involve all stakeholders: Involve all stakeholders, including employees, customers, and vendors, in the continuous improvement process to gain insights and perspectives from different angles.

Implement changes incrementally: Implement changes incrementally to avoid overwhelming employees and ensure that changes are manageable.

Monitor and adapt: Monitor the results of changes and adapt strategies as needed to ensure that the business continues to improve.

Invest in training and development: Invest in employee training and development to build skills and knowledge that can contribute to continuous improvement.

By implementing these strategies, businesses can create a culture of continuous improvement and position themselves for long-term success and growth.

Role of technology in streamlining operations and improving efficiency

Technology plays a critical role in streamlining operations and improving efficiency in modern businesses. Here are some ways that technology can help:

Automation: Technology can automate many business processes, including data entry, customer service, and inventory management. Automation can reduce errors, save time, and increase productivity.

Collaboration: Technology can facilitate collaboration among team members, departments, and even with external stakeholders. With tools like cloud-based collaboration software and video conferencing, teams can work together regardless of location, making it easier to share information and ideas.

Data analytics: Technology allows businesses to collect and analyze large amounts of data, which can be used to identify trends, make informed decisions, and optimize operations.

Customer engagement: Technology can help businesses engage with customers in new and innovative ways, including through social media, email marketing, and personalized promotions.

Mobile technology: Mobile devices and apps can help employees stay connected and productive while on-the-go, increasing efficiency and flexibility.

E-commerce: Technology enables businesses to sell their products and services online, opening up new markets and revenue streams.

Cloud computing: Cloud-based systems can provide businesses with access to the latest software and hardware without the need for expensive infrastructure investments.

By leveraging technology, businesses can improve operational efficiency, reduce costs, and better serve customers. However, it is important to remember that technology is a tool, and it is critical to have the right processes and people in place to maximize its benefits.

Conclusion

Key takeaways from the book

The book covers a range of topics related to business and entrepreneurship, including creating a business plan, identifying target markets, assessing competition, marketing strategies, sales techniques, leadership skills, operations management, and continuous improvement. Here are some key takeaways from the book:

Having a clear vision and mission is essential to creating a successful business.

Market research is critical to understanding your target market and competition.

There are several business structures to choose from, each with its own pros and cons.

Funding options for startups include loans, crowdfunding, and angel investors.

Marketing is important for attracting and retaining customers, and strategies such as social media, email marketing, and content marketing can be effective.

A strong brand identity and messaging can help differentiate your business and create customer loyalty.

Sales techniques include prospecting, qualifying leads, building rapport, and overcoming objections.

Customer relationship management is crucial for building long-term relationships and generating repeat business.

Effective leadership requires traits and skills such as communication, delegation, decision-making, and emotional intelligence.

Continuous improvement is essential for staying competitive and adapting to changing business environments.

Technology can help streamline operations and improve efficiency in areas such as automation, collaboration, data analytics, customer engagement, mobile technology, e-commerce, and cloud computing.

By implementing these strategies and techniques, entrepreneurs and business owners can build successful businesses and achieve their goals.

Final words of advice and encouragement to readers starting or growing their businesses

Starting or growing a business can be challenging, but it can also be incredibly rewarding. Here are some final words of advice and encouragement for readers:

Believe in yourself and your vision. Stay focused and persistent, and don't be discouraged by setbacks or failures.

Surround yourself with a supportive network of mentors, advisors, and peers who can provide guidance and feedback.

Take the time to develop a comprehensive business plan, and be open to revising it as your business evolves.

Stay agile and adaptable, and be willing to pivot your strategies and tactics as needed.

Stay up-to-date on industry trends and best practices, and continue to learn and develop new skills.

Build a strong team of employees who share your vision and values, and invest in their growth and development.

Remember to take care of yourself and prioritize your physical and mental health. Running a business can be stressful, so it's important to practice self-care and find ways to recharge and stay motivated.

Above all, remember that entrepreneurship is a journey, and there will be ups and downs along the way. Stay true to your vision and values, and keep pushing forward towards your goals. With hard work, dedication, and a bit of luck, you can achieve success and build a thriving business.